The Way of
THE SEA

TIMOTHY FREKE

A GODSFIELD BOOK

INTRODUCTION

I t is a deeply spiritual experience to stand by the sea and
sense its power; to see it stretching to the horizon and
be awed by its scope and beauty. The immense oceans
clothe the Earth. From outer space ours is a blue planet. Is
it more than a remarkable coincidence that the percentage
of our home world covered by the seas is the same as the
percentage of water in a human body? We are water
beings. To commune with the sea is to experience the
primal home of all life forms, from which all creatures
have evolved.

Yet the sea is mighty and fearful. It is the tomb of
countless anonymous adventures. It rages and gales. Its
water cannot quench our thirst. Its depths are dark and
secret places. We know more about the moon than these
unfathomable worlds. We have crossed the oceans but have
not tamed them. The sea is still wild. Perhaps that is why
to stand by her shores, where the winds blow and the
spume hisses, is to feel truly free; to know that we will pass
like the crashing waves and another will rise behind us,
while the tides roll in and out for all eternity.

THE MYSTICAL SEA

THE VAST OCEAN is a perennial image of the all encompassing nature of God. The great Hindu mystic Sankara described Brahman, the ineffable Oneness of God, as an ocean of endless joy. The Ashtavakra Gita, a Hindu scripture, points toward our essential shared identity as the Atman – a limitless sea of Being on which individual selves rise and fall like waves. The Buddha compares the experience of enlightenment to a drop of water merging with the sea from which it came. The Taoist Lao Tzu sees himself on a journey back to the Tao, the primal Source, like a river rushing to the sea. Yet these images do not suffice to convey the sublime nature of the Truth the mystics have experienced. Like the frog in a traditional Hindu teaching story, all the mystics can ultimately do is encourage us to experience the ocean of God for ourselves.

Following Tao in the world
is as natural as a mountain stream,
that becomes part of a valley brook,
that becomes part of a great river,
that flows to the One Sea.

LAO TZU

As rivers flow into the sea

and in so doing lose name and form,

so the wise, who are free from name and form,

reach the Supreme Being,

the Self-luminous, the Infinite.

Someone who knows Brahman

becomes Brahman.

MUNDAKA UPANISHAD

Streams and rivers flow to the sea,

because it lies below them.

That's why it is the greatest body of water.

Following this example,

the wise are always humble.

LAO TZU

My mind fell like a hailstone into the vast expanse of Brahman's ocean. Touching one drop of it, I melted away and became one with Brahman. This is wonderful indeed! Here is the ocean of Brahman, full of endless joy. How can I accept or reject anything? Is there anything distinct from Brahman? Now, finally and clearly, I know that I am the Atman, the One Soul, whose nature is eternal bliss. I see nothing. I hear nothing. I know nothing that is separate from me.

SANKARA

I am the breathing wind

and the ocean waves.

I am the sun's bright rays,

and the sparkling stars.

I am the rustling leaves,

and the power that brings

the bud into blossom.

I am the salmon swimming,

the brave boar fighting,

the fast stag running,

the strong ox pulling,

the mighty oak standing.

I am the thoughts of everyone,

who praises my exquisite beauty.

THE CELTIC CHRISTIAN
BLACK BOOK OF CARMARTHEN

O, the wonder that I am! I salute myself who, though with a body, am one who neither goes anywhere nor comes from anywhere but ever abides pervading the universe.

O, in Me the limitless ocean! The movement of the mind has produced the many worlds like the wind produces diverse waves on the ocean.

How remarkable! In Me the limitless ocean. The waves of individual selves rise according to their inherent nature, meet and play with one another for a while and then disappear.

ASHTAVAKRA GITA

The cycle of reincarnation is like the water cycle.
Water evaporates into nothingness and then falls as droplets
from the heavens, like the individual souls incarnating here
on earth – only to make their way via streams and rivers to
the mighty sea, and to be evaporated once again by the
great spiritual sun into nothingness.

SHEN HSUI

All the rivers run into the sea,
yet it is not full;
unto the place from whence the rivers run,
thither they return again.

ECCLESIASTES

A toad who lived in a well was one day visited by a toad who lived in the sea. "How big is your well?" asked the first toad. "Is it as big as mine?" The sea toad smiled and tried to explain, "My well is so huge that it has no edges. It contains so much water that it could never run dry in a million hot summers. It is so deep that perhaps it has no bottom." The first toad looked incredulous. "You are either boasting or your imagination has run away with itself!" he complained. "Come with me," said the sea toad, "and I will show you."

HINDU TEACHING STORY

What am I? What are you? We are all aspects of the one sea of Being. Our lives are the rising and falling of a passing wave on the eternal ocean which, in truth, we are.

ISSA DAS

Don't think that saying "I am God" is proclaiming one's greatness. It is actually total humility. Someone who says "I am the servant of God" infers two – God and himself – whereas someone who says "I am God" negates himself. He relinquishes his own existence. "I am God" means "I don't exist. Everything is God. Only God exists. I am nothing. I am utter emptiness." This is complete humility not arrogance, but people often misunderstand. When someone says that he is God's servant, he still sees himself as a "doer", albeit in God's service. He is not yet drowned in the ocean of God. When he is, there will be no such thing as "his actions," only movements of the water.

JALALUDIN RUMI

The liberated soul loses her name in the One

through Whom and in Whom she merges;

just as a river reaching the sea

loses the identity with which it flowed

through many countries

to arrive at this destination.

Now it is in the sea

and here it rests without labor.

MARGUERITE PORETE

*H*is will is the ocean into which

all streams and currents pour.

ALIGHIERI DANTE

Time is like a bubble on the ocean of eternity. Before the bubble was in existence the ocean was there, and after the bubble bursts the ocean will be there still.

DR. CHRISTIE

You are a droplet of water from an infinite ocean of consciousness.

HAJI BAHAUDIN

You are a fish swimming
in an ocean of God.

SAI BABA

When I hear that a fish in the ocean is thirsty,

I have to laugh.

Life itself lives in your own home –

and you just don't get it.

You walk from one sacred site to another,

looking permanently perplexed.

Kabir will tell you how it is:

Go wherever you want,

to Calcutta or distant Tibet,

if you can't find the hiding place of your soul

this world will never be real for you.

KABIR

THE SPIRITUAL SEA

THE SEA is a teacher with much wisdom to impart. Like life itself, she washes all before her. She speaks with many voices: the low growl of the breakers on the rock; the gentle hiss as she caresses soft sand; the mournful cry of her seagulls; the thunderous cacophony of her angry storms. Each voice has spoken to some witness of the grandeur and depths of life, of immortality; of a power more permanent than our own transitory existence. What greater reminder is there of the awesome mystery that surrounds us everywhere than the endless sea, playfully splashing and murderously raging?

He that will learn to pray, let him go to the sea.

GEORGE HERBERT

They that go down to the sea in ships,
that do business in great waters;

these see the works of the Lord,
and his wonders in the deep.

PSALM 107

$\mathcal{N}$ow I perceive that I have not understood anything –
not a single object – and that no man ever can.
I perceive Nature, here in sight of the sea, is taking advantage
of me, to dart upon me, and sting me,
Because I have dared to open my mouth and sing at all.

WALT WHITMAN

God alone can fully and always hear the voice that the earth utters to the sky the many tongues of its many waters. But He sends us men sometimes to whom He has given such ears in their soul that they can perceive some of the meaning of the world's great sea voice, and they are able to translate for us some of the music and the magic of the sea-soul of the earth. These men are poets or painters, or musicians, and they can hear more than most of us, far more than we hear at the coast, of the great sea's musical mystery, the strange trouble of the weird waters, and the moving ocean's mighty joy. And they sing for us, these men, what the sea says, and their voice is beautiful and wonderful.

J.P. FORSYTH

Thou paragon of elemental powers,

Mystery of water – never slumbering sea!

Impassioned orator with lips sublime,

Whose waves are arguments which prove a God!

ROBERT MONTGOMERY

Hence in a season of calm weather,

Though inland far we be,

Our souls have sight of that immortal sea,

Which brought us hither,

Can in a moment travel thither,

And hear the mighty waters rolling evermore.

WILLIAM WORDSWORTH

As I wend to the shores I know not,

As I list to the dirge, the voices of men and
women wrecked,

As I inhale the impalpable breezes that set in
upon me,

As the ocean so mysterious rolls towards me
closer and closer,

I too but signify, at the utmost, a little
washed-up drift,

A few sands and dead leaves to gather,

Gather, and merge myself as part of the
sands and drift.

WALT WHITMAN

Those overtaken by a storm when traveling by sea don't worry about their luggage, but throw it overboard with their own hands, considering their property to be less important than their lives. So why don't we, following their example, throw out whatever drags our soul down to the depths.

ST. NELIOS THE ASCETIC

The sea reflects the sun perfectly if the water is still. But if it is agitated by the wind the light fragments into a million mirrored suns. It is like this with the mind. If the mind is disturbed by thoughts, the Light of Oneness is fragmented and we perceive only the manyness of things. When thoughts are still, however, the One Light is perfectly reflected in the mind.

ISSA DAS

Imagine an ox's yoke adrift on the vast ocean and a turtle happening to poke its head through the hole – this is how rare and extra- ordinary it is to be born a human being.

KUNKYEN LONGCHEN RABJAM

If you would swim on the bosom
of the ocean of Truth,
you must reduce yourself to a zero.

MAHAIMA GANDHI

*I*n China there once lived a wrestler called
"Great Waves." He was immensely strong
and in practice sessions always won his contests.
But in public he always failed. Great Waves
went to Hakuju, a Zen master, for help. The
master advised, "Great Waves" is your name, so
stay in the temple tonight and imagine that you
are the huge billowing sea, swallowing all in its
path — unstoppable!" The wrestler meditated all
night in the temple. At first he was distracted,
but gradually he saw himself as a mighty wave
— becoming larger and larger. Soon the shrine
and the statue of the Buddha were swept away

before him — the whole temple became the ebb

and flow of the sea. In the morning Hakuju

found him faintly smiling. He patted the wrestler

on the shoulders and said, "You are those waves.

You will sweep all before you." After that no

wrestler could ever defeat Great Waves.

ZEN TEACHING STORY

The ancient philosopher Diagoras the Cynic was admiring with a friend the many votive monuments to the gods surrounding a temple. His friend explained to him that these structures had been erected out of gratitude by those who, whilst in peril on the sea, had promised to honor the gods if divine intervention rescued them from a watery grave. The monuments were testimony to the efficacy of prayer and the power of the gods. Diagoras replied sardonically, "Just think how many more there would have been if all those who had drowned had also been able to set one up."

CICERO

Diagoras was on a voyage when the sea became very rough. The nervous crew began muttering that it was because they were carrying on board someone who ridiculed the gods as religious superstition. Pointing out other ships also caught in the same storm, Diagoras muttered, "How remarkable! If you are right, every one of these vessels must also be carrying a Diagoras as a passenger."

CICERO

Love still has something
of the sea.

SIR CHARLES SIDNEY

OCEAN OF LOVE

THE MANY MOODS of the ocean have offered poets a constant source of evocative imagery for the life of the passions – especially love. Whether it be love of another or ecstatic love of God, poets and mystics turn to metaphors of the sea to express their obsessive ardor. Aphrodite, the Greek goddess of love and desire, was born from the sea. She rose naked from the spume riding a scallop shell and was known as "the foam-born." She came from the chaos and danced on the shores. To experience the love she inspires is to be lost in an ocean of bliss. To be abandoned by love is to feel adrift in a small boat, tossed by currents beyond any control. Our emotions, like the ocean, are delightful and destructive. But without them it would be a dry world.

The bridegroom sea
Is toying with the shore, his wedded bride,
And in the fullness of his marriage joy
He decorates her tawny brow with shells,
Retires a pace to see how fair she looks,
Then, proud, runs up to kiss her.

ALEXANDER SMITH

Unchangeable, save to thy wild wave's play;

Time writes no wrinkle on thine azure brow,

Such as creation's dawn beheld, thou rollest now.

Thou glorious mirror, where the Almighty's form

Glasses itself in tempests, in all time,

Calm or convulsed, in breeze, or gale, or storm,

Icing the pole, or in the torrid clime,

Dark-heaving – boundless, endless, and sublime,

The image of eternity, the throne

Of the Invisible; even from out thy slime

The monsters of the deep are made; each zone

Obeys thee; thou goest forth, dread, fathomless, alone.

And I have loved thee, Ocean!

GEORGE GORDON, LORD BYRON

Soothe! soothe! soothe!
Close on each wave soothes the wave behind,
And again another behind, embracing and
             lapping, everyone close –
But my love soothes not me, not me.

Low hangs the moon – it rose late;
O it is lagging – O I think it is heavy with
             love, with love.

O madly the sea pushes, pushes upon
             the land, with love – with love.
O night! do I not see my love fluttering out there
             amongst the breakers?
What is that little black thing I see there in the white?

Loud! loud! loud!
Loud I call to you, my love!
High and clear I shoot my voice over the waves;
Surely you must know who is here, is here;
You must know who I am, my love.

WALT WHITMAN

My tossing mind
becomes becalmed
as you walk
across its waters.

ISSA DAS

My soul is an enchanted boat,

Which like a sleeping swan, doth float,

upon the silver waves of thy sweet singing.

PERCY BYSSHE SHELLEY

I navigate serious seas

only soothed by your smile.

Be my lifeboat

and my star to guide it.

Only you can bring me home,

for you are where my heart is.

Issa Das

Many waves cannot quench love,
Nor can the flood drown it out.

THE SONG OF SOLOMON

Like as the waves make towards the pebbled shore

So do our minutes hasten to their end;

Each changing place with that which goes before,

In sequent toil all forwards do contend.

Nativity, once in the main of light,

Crawls to maturity, wherewith being crowned,

Crooked eclipses 'gainst his glory fight,

And Time that gave doth now his gift confound.

Time doth transfix the flourish set on youth

And delves the parallels in beauty's brow,

Feeds on the rarities of nature's truth,

And nothing stands but for his scythe to mow,

And yet to time in hope my verse shall stand,

Praising thy worth, despite his cruel hand.

WILLIAM SHAKESPEARE

*O*ne day I wrote her name upon the sand,

But came the waves and washed it away.

Again I wrote it with a second hand,

But came in the sand and made my

pains his prey. Vain man said she, that

dost vain assay, a mortal thing so to immortalize.

EMILY DICKINSON

The milky way is as flotsam
on the vast ocean of ecstatic love.

JALALUDIN RUMI

Imagine Brahman as a sea without shores.
Through the cooling love of the devotee some
of the water becomes frozen into blocks of ice.
Now and then, God assumes a form and reveals
Himself to his lovers as a person. But when the sun of
Knowledge rises the blocks of ice melt away and God
is without form, no more a person. He is beyond
description. Who could describe Him? Anyone who
tries disappears, unable to find his "I" anymore.

RAMAKRISHNA

Chained by love.
Captured again.
Struggle is futile.
Escape is impossible.

Love is a sea
with unseen shores —
with no shores at all.
The wary don't dive in.
To swim in love
is to drink poison
and find it sweet.

I struggled like a wild mare
drawing the noose tighter.

RABI'A

*M*y brimming heart

held whole in full embrace,

flotsam upon the tides of breath,

washed in taste, splashed by spume of light,

tossed by Tao's undulant pulse,

born on swells of simple love,

falling into waiting arms,

surging up from depths of bliss.

Eroded by the turmoil of your ocean presence,

waves of ringing break on rough rocks,

sucking back smooth pebbles,

grinding grit to soft sand,

dissolving my grateful heart in your bounty.

ISSA DAS

Why should we ever part – we two?

Like the leaves of a plant floating on the waters –

we live as the Great One and the small one.

Like the owl gazing all night at the moon –

We live as the Great One and the small one.

This love cannot end –

it goes back to the very first lovers.

This is what Kabir says:

Just as river water becomes sea water,

You and I are indivisible.

KABIR

If all the land were turned to paper
and all the seas to ink,
and all the forests into pens to write with,
they would still not suffice
to describe the greatness of the guru.

KABIR

SEA OF IMAGES

THE GREAT PSYCHOLOGIST Carl Jung compared the "collective unconscious" to the sea. To dream of the sea is to encounter the hidden depths we share. The ocean contains images, as rich as sunken treasure, that question and inform our terrestrial existence. Her metaphors are as fluid as her currents, defying the limitations of the rational mind and exciting the poetic imagination. To some she whispers "life" to others "death" yet contained in both is the silent message "mystery". Her roar drowns out the chatter of the trivial mind, and in that white noise can be heard the secret silence of the soul.

To me the sea is a continual miracle;

The fishes that swim

– the rocks

– the motion of the waves

– the ships with men in them,

What stranger miracles are there?

WALT WHITMAN

One bright morning in mid-ocean I looked off upon the water and it was so calm and bright I said "This is the infinite smile of an infinite God." Then again in the summer time, strolling near the beach in the darkness, I heard the voice of the waters, and I said, "This is the long metre psalm of the deep."

TALMAGE

*I*t is not by descriptions

that the magic of the sea

can be brought before the reader's mind.

This can only be achieved

by the unconscious touch

of one between whom and the sea

there exists a sympathy

as rare as it is mysterious.

There are but few who know

how the beauty of every other object of nature

is increased and intensified

as soon as ever it touches the sea.

There are but few who really feel

how the joyful news of sunrise,

is never fully and finally proclaimed

till the sea has owned it,

caught it, tossed it from wave to wave.

There are but few who really feel

that the silent message of the moon

is never so eloquent in its silence

as when translated by the rippling disk

that answers it in the bosom of the sea.

There are few that really feel

that the calm stars are never so full

with comfort to a soul in sorrow,

and that the bright cloud-pageantry

of a summer noon is never so joyful

to a soul in joy, as when all these riches

of the earth and air live a larger and fuller life

in the mirror that girdles the world.

ATHEOUM

Some people call the great world God's cathedral.

Well one of its organs is the sea.

Oh it is a great organ the sea!

It can play as sweet and soft as a flute.

But it can also roar and thunder to terrify the bravest.

It is awful to hear the sea rolling in like mountains

upon a shore of rocks and caves,

and rousing echoes which are heard far inland

as if many giants were roaring into many tunes.

I suppose it is very silent at the bottom of the sea.

The fishes and the shells may know nothing

of all the concert amid which they live.

But we can hear it, though we can hardly tell the words it sings.

We can hear its music, so strange,

mysterious, magical, and mighty.

There are some hearts it can speak to, and they know what it says.

They listen and they are soothed;

or they listen and they feel something like rapture;

or as they listen they feel something like terror,

but always they love as they listen

to the many sounds and the one great voice.

REV. P.T. FORSYTH

The world is too much with us; late and soon,

Getting and spending, we lay waste our powers,

Little we see in Nature which is ours;

We have given our hearts away, a sordid boon!

This sea that bares her bosom to the moon;

The winds that will be howling at all hours,

And are up-gathered now like sleeping flowers;

For this, for everything, we are out of tune;

It moves us not, Great God! I'd rather be

A Pagan suckled in a creed outworn;

So might I, standing on this pleasant lea,

Have glimpses that would make me less forlorn;

Have sight of Proteus coming from the sea;

Or hear old Triton blow his wreathed horn

WILLIAM WORDSWORTH

There is a tide in the affairs of men,
Which, taken at the flood, leads on to fortune;
Omitted, all the voyage of their life,
Is bound in shallows, and in miseries:
And we must take the current when it serves,
Or lose our ventures.

WILLIAM SHAKESPEARE

*T*he sea is the largest of all cemeteries,

and its slumberers sleep without monuments.

All other graveyards, in all other lands,

show some symbol of distinction

between the great and the small, the rich and poor;

but in that ocean cemetery, the king and the clown,

the prince and the peasant, are alike distinguished.

The same waves roll over all, the same requiem

by the minstrels of the ocean is sung to their honor.

Over their remains the same storm beats,

and the same sun shines; and there, unmarked,

the weak and the powerful, the plumed and the unhonored,

will sleep on until awakened by the same trump,

when the sea shall give up its dead.

MANTELL

The dim, dark sea,
so like unto Death,
That divides and yet
unites mankind!

HENRY WADSWORTH LONGFELLOW

Whereto answering the sea,

delaying not, hurrying not,

Whispered me through the night,

      and very plainly before daybreak,

Lisped to me the low and delicious word DEATH;

And again Death – ever Death, Death, Death,

Hissing melodious, neither like the bird

      nor like my aroused child's heart,

But edging near, as privately for me, rustling at my feet,

creeping thence steadily up to my ears,

      and loving me softly all over,

Death, Death, Death, Death, Death.

My own songs awakened from that hour;

And with them the key, the word up from the waves,

The word of the sweetest song, and all songs,

That strong and delicious word which, creeping to my feet,

The Sea whispered me.

WALT WHITMAN

Library of Congress Cataloging-in-Publication Data Available

10 9 8 7 6 5 4 3 2 1

Published in 1998 by Sterling Publishing Company, Inc.
387 Park Avenue South, New York, N.Y. 10016

© 1998 GODSFIELD PRESS

Text © 1998 Timothy Freke

Produced for Sterling Publishing by
Godsfield Press Limited

Designed by the
Bridgewater Book Company

Distributed in Canada by Sterling Publishing
c/o Canadian Manda Group, One Atlantic Avenue, Suite 105
Toronto, Ontario, Canada M6K 3E7

Distributed in Australia by Capricorn Link (Australia) Pty Ltd
P O. Box 6651, Baulkham Hills, Business Centre, NSW 2153, Australia

Printed and bound in Hong Kong

ISBN 0-8069-2051-3

The publisher would like to thank that following for the use of pictures:

Fine Art Photographic Library, The Stock Market

Author's Acknowledgments

My thanks to Deborah O'Shea, and Ellen and John Freke,
for all their help in compiling this little book.